How to Run Music Group Rehearsals

Janet Goepel
University Tutor in Education

John Leach
Retired Minister in the Church of England
and University Tutor

GROVE BOOKS LIMITED
RIDLEY HALL RD CAMBRIDGE CB3 9HU

Contents

Authors' Note

We first met in 1985 in a church in Sheffield, and began to collaborate together in what became an exciting and creative music group. During this time we worked with many different and gifted musicians, developing and teaching a strategy for running enjoyable and efficient practice sessions. We then went our separate ways, John to be a vicar and Janet to become a university lecturer, but we each remained involved with the musical life of different churches. We have now met up again nearly 40 years on, and have decided that the material we used in the 1980s, suitably updated in the light of our own experiences, might be useful for a wider audience, so the result is this book. Come and see.

Acknowledgments

As usual we would like to thank the members of GROW for their faith in, and help with, this project, particularly Pete Gunstone and Anne Harrison who provided helpful comments on the text.

First Impression November 2023
ISSN 0144-1728
ISBN 978 1 78827 351 0

1 Introduction

The way we live our lives today seems to be about being busy. Ask almost anyone how they are, and invariably they will answer 'Busy!' As a result of this we are often looking for ways in which we can save time, or we only manage the immediate. Practising music for services can often be squeezed into the hour before the service. This of itself puts limitations on how prepared the musicians are for worship and on how well they can prepare the music. It also puts the musicians under pressure, as there is a defined time by which they need to have concluded their preparation, whether that preparation is sufficient or not. This booklet aims to encourage those involved in leading music in churches to conduct effective rehearsals. It outlines why this is important and offers ideas and suggestions about how this can be done and enjoyed. You will soon see that our primary focus in this book is worship bands and so-called contemporary worship, but there will be some principles along the way which will be applicable to other groupings such as choirs. We are also aware that some churches will have singing groups who would not identify as robed choirs, but equally do not contain instrumentalists. We hope there will also be useful principles for such groups.

Vision and Culture

Each church has its own distinct culture. This depends on many factors such as its geographical location, the composition and age of the congregation, the church style or tradition and so on. It is important for the musicians to ensure they know how the leaders of the church understand the role of music in services and seek to work within that. If the leaders do not seem to know how to articulate their vision for music in the church, then working together to define the vision would be ideal.

Once a vision is understood, then music can be chosen and prepared in a way which aligns with that vision. If there is a difference of opinion between the music leader and the church leader about the vision, then this needs to be worked through to a place of common understanding, otherwise there is likely to be constant friction.[1] As part of the dialogue with the church leader, there should be an agreement about who chooses the material to be sung at services. If this is the music leader, then the church leader needs to provide some guidance about readings, liturgy, sermon themes or other helpful information to support appropriate musical choices. On one occasion, Janet recalls being asked to provide music for a service, so she requested further information about the kind of song expected at a particular point in the service. The church leader's reply was, 'I don't know, but I will know when I see it.' Perhaps a little more guidance than this would have been beneficial.

Relationships

Conducting rehearsals during the week prior to the Sunday service also provides an opportunity for relationships to grow and develop. Deeper relationships provide an atmosphere of trust which allows musicians to try something new without fear of failure or embarrassment. It provides the opportunity for the music leader to give encouragement and, when needed, honest feedback. It means that an attitude of servanthood can be encouraged, where not everyone plays everything all the time. Solo instruments, in particular, can come in and out at various points in a song or hymn and provide enhancement which could heighten the words being sung and thereby support the congregation in how they respond to the sung material.

Additionally, having a gap between the rehearsal and the Sunday service, with scope for individual practice between the two, provides an opportunity for the learning from the rehearsal to move from working memory to long-term memory. Neuroscience considers that working memory is about temporary activation of neurons in the brain, whereas long-term memory occurs because of physical changes to neurons and their connections. These changes occur through repetition and practice, so giving more time for rehearsal enables the musicians to be more secure in what they play and sing at the service, as they will have activated their long-term memory. This, incidentally, is why it is important to make sure that the service has within it well-known songs and hymns from time to time, as this involves those whose memories are no longer able to make connections with new learning.

Why Rehearse?

For anyone to become competent in an instrument or voice requires practice. Those who have been involved in any kind of musical activity will understand how important it is to be able to master your instrument or voice beyond being a beginner. Rehearsal, then, needs to begin at an individual level. This does not necessarily mean that you have to learn musical notation, although that can be very helpful. Some musicians can play or sing well by ear. Indeed, the way songs are often learned in church contexts, especially when using a band, is through repeated listening to songs on Spotify or YouTube.

Different Types of Notation for Worship Bands

There are four main ways in which music is notated. The first is formal musical notation, like this, which may or may not have added guitar chord symbols:

The second is known as a 'lead sheet,' with the melody and chords only:

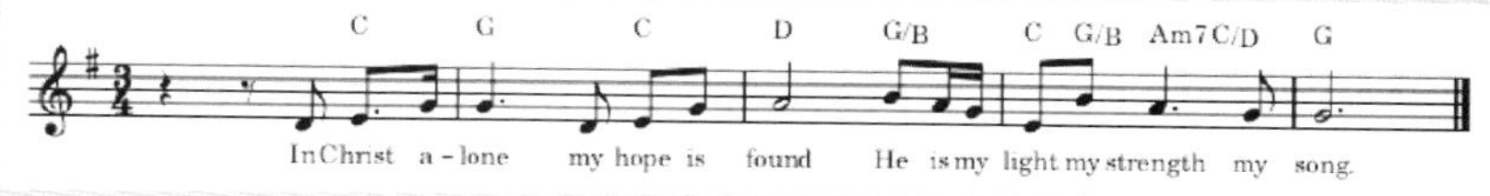

The third, the 'chord sheet' is simply words with chords:

C G C D G/B C G/B Am7 C/DG
In Christ a-lone my hope is found He is my light, my strength, my song

The fourth, for more advanced musicians, is 'figured notation' which, rather than using chord names uses their degrees in the scale of the key in which the piece is written. The advantage of this is that a song can be played in any key, if musicians are familiar with the chords in a variety of keys. This convention would look like this:

IV I IV V Ib IV Ib IIm V7d I
In Christ a-lone my hope is found He is my light, my strength, my song

'Inversions' of chords are indicated by the small letters 'b' and 'd' above, where b is the first inversion (2nd note of the triad in the bass), and d the 3rd inversion (4th note in the bass).

Assuming those who are involved in leading worship through music in church are competent in their instrument or voice, this then frees up the band or choir time for learning how to play or sing *together*. Learning to play and/or sing with others is vitally important, whatever the level of skill, particularly if the composition of the band is different each time. Playing or singing with the same group of people enables each person to understand their role in relation to others. If, however, the composition of the group varies from one time to the next, then individual and collective rehearsal time in advance is even more crucial. This gives time for the people involved to get to know each other and the extent of their competence, as well as to play to each other's strengths. Additionally, taking time to rehearse with any technology (sound and/or projected words) which might be used is also important. Having the tech team involved in the rehearsal pays dividends during the service, as they can more readily anticipate what the band is going to do and support them better, thus serving the congregation better too.

Using Practice Time

2

Our experience of different churches suggests that the practice or rehearsal time, if indeed there is any, consists of playing through the songs which are going to be used on the following Sunday. There might be other ingredients, like an opening prayer, vocal warm-ups or some social space, but the bulk of the time is spent on what we will call 'maintenance,' keeping things going for the immediate task in hand. This is represented in the first diagram below. However, we became frustrated with this approach, as it contained no time for, or expectation of, any development, in other words working on material which we would not be using in the immediate future. Realizing that this was a recipe for stagnation, we began a policy of dividing our time in half, and building in development time as well as the necessary maintenance. Eventually this model evolved into the second diagram which will form the basis of the material in this book.

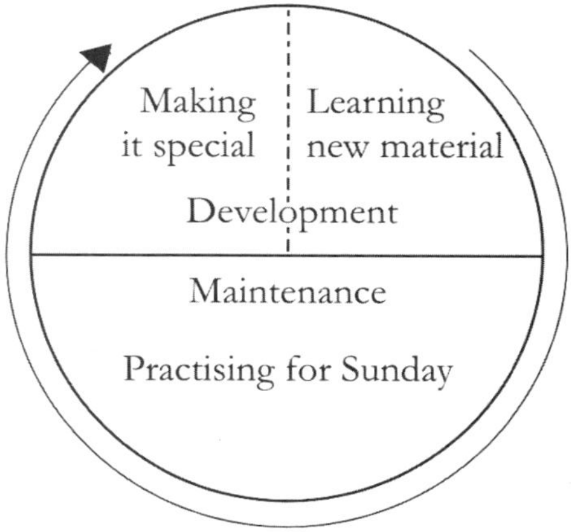

The time below the horizontal diameter is the Maintenance section, with Development above it. This time, in turn, is divided between the initial learning of new material, and creative work on songs we already know. Each of these three sections will be explained more fully as we go along. The logical flow of this book, therefore, starts at the top right of the circle and moves clockwise around it, from learning new songs to using them well, and then exploring whether we might do things even better. The 'Development' chapter, therefore, is split into two parts, either side of the chapter on 'Maintenance.'

Three initial points need to be made. The first is that the diagram represents time allocation, but it should not be seen as inflexible. It is not meant to tie you in to using a two-hour practice for one hour's practice for Sunday, then half an hour each of learning and creativity. Some weeks will require more maintenance than others, and we certainly would not recommend weekly new material. So think of the diagram as representing time allocation over, say, six months rather than one week. However, *any* time spent on some development might be an improvement for groups which only ever prepare for the upcoming service. Maintenance is greedy, and should not be allowed to take over.

Maintenance is greedy, and should not be allowed to take over

Secondly, it is worth remembering that rehearsal can take place at three levels, and while we will concentrate mainly on the second, a diagram like this can equally apply to all three. The first is one's individual practice at home during the week. As musicians we wither and die if we stop practising our instruments or voices, and we cheat other musicians as well as the congregation if we turn up unprepared. Band rehearsals are not the time for practising individual parts. Secondly there is the rehearsal itself, and this will form the main focus of this book. But thirdly there might be practices with the musicians along with the tech team, which introduces a further dynamic. To see our diagram as a potential model for all three levels could be a helpful way to proceed.

The third comment is really about your context. We are aware that a vast range of different musicians with different abilities are involved in leading worship, from hi-tech rock bands to robed choirs with two members attempting to sing four-part harmony (yes, John really had this in one of his churches). We have tried to write from somewhere in the centre of these two extremes. However, it would help you, dear reader, to try and extract some *principles* which would work for you, rather than discarding the book because you do not have any trombone players, or whatever. Things like agreeing which key you are in, and knowing how and when to come in together are applicable across the spectrum, even if some parts of our book feel either above you or way below you. We are aware we might already have alienated some of you because the furthest your 'tech' goes is lifting the lid on the piano. So please forgive us when our writing misses the target for you, and try to identify some underlying principles from which you might nevertheless learn. We are unashamedly writing in pursuit of excellence, but maybe you could find some snippets which could lead to improvement.

Development Part 1: Learning New Material

3

There is great benefit in using the familiar as this enables the congregation to sing with confidence, but of course it is also helpful to introduce new material from time to time. The frequency at which new material is introduced often depends on the type of music usually used, the nature of the congregation, the musicians themselves and the style of the service the music is for. Some churches use sung settings for liturgy led by a choir, which the congregation knows well. Others have little set liturgy but choose songs relevant to a particular part of the service (such as confession, praise) or which relate to the sermon. Still other churches seem to use songs that are currently popular, that excite or prompt an emotional response. These songs may or may not be related to any theme within the service itself. All of this raises the question as to what songs or hymns might be introduced as new, first to the musicians and then eventually to the congregation.

What Songs or Hymns Should I Choose?

In selecting new material, the music leader needs to know why it is being introduced, whether it is singable by this particular congregation and whether it is appropriate for the style of service or meeting usual for their own congregational context. A helpful discussion on how to select new material can be found in Mark Earey's booklet and so will not be discussed here.[2] For an analysis of the difference between hymns and worship songs, see John's previous Grove booklet.[3]

Working with a Repertoire

Most popular hymn books have between 600 and 1000 hymns in them, of which probably no more than perhaps 100 are known and sung regularly. Similarly the CCLI database includes around 100,000 songs. This can provide an overwhelming amount of choice, so in parish ministry John worked with a deliberate repertoire approach. Each year a team would list around 100 songs and a similar number of hymns which we would use in our worship. This list was updated annually, and songs (but fewer hymns) would drop off the bottom of the list. Usually this was because they had passed their worship-by date, and would be replaced by a similar number of new songs. Only material on the repertoire was allowed. On the rare occasions when we used a song which nobody knew (because the words fitted so well, or because someone had enjoyed it at a conference), it usually flopped and reinforced the idea that a prescribed repertoire was a good and useful thing. We commend it to you.

Becoming Familiar with a New Song or Hymn

Once the music leader has decided on a new song or hymn, it needs to be introduced first to the musicians and then to the congregation. New material can be learned within the context of the music rehearsal in a number of ways. This can depend on different musicians' competence, how they prefer to learn, and whether or not they can access musical notation. The box below summarizes different conventions for notation.

Understanding Chord Notation

As we have seen, chord sheets have the words with guitar chords written above them, in the places where the chords change. There are different conventions for chord notation, but as a general rule...

A is an A major triad (1st, 3rd and 5th of the scale, or A - C# - E).

Am is a minor triad (A - C - E).

A7 adds the flattened seventh note of the scale (A - C# - E - G).

Am7 adds the flattened seventh to the minor triad (A - C - E - G).

A° is the diminished chord which contains A (A - C - Eb/D# - Gb/F#).

Sometimes you will want a different note in the bass, and not simply the bottom note of the triad. This is written **Am7/G**, and is called 'A minor 7 over G.'

Note that chord notation gives you no information at all about how the tune goes.

Interval terminology: each note of the major scale has a name, which will be the same whatever the starting note of the scale. The ones which are most common in worship music are the *Tonic* (1st note, I), *Subdominant* (4th, IV), *Dominant* (5th, V) and *Submediant* (6th, VI). So a *Dominant 7th* (V7) is the fifth note of the scale, with the flattened seventh note added to the triad of 1st, 3rd and 5th. So in the key of E, the dominant 7th would be B7 (B - D# - F# - A).

There is much more to it than this, so why not use some of your development time now and again for someone who understands all this to teach some basics to those who have not learnt to read music?

Having decided which notation is best for you as a team, then you can use any of the following approaches to learn the song:

- The music leader teaches the song directly to the singers, perhaps using a combination of written music and rote learning;
- The music leader may provide written harmonies, or may expect the singers to improvise them;
- The music leader or individuals may provide written band parts for solo instruments, especially for transposing instruments such as clarinets or trumpets;
- The music leader provides simple music copies and expects solo instrumentalists to improvise their own part;
- Music is learnt aurally from recordings such as on YouTube;
- There is no clear focus to learning new material and everyone just plays and sings as they wish.

Introducing New Material—A Four-stage Process

Introducing a new song should be done well in advance of it being needed for the congregation in a service. From her experience, Janet therefore proposes a four-stage process for introducing new material for congregational use:

1. The musicians are introduced to the new song or hymn in rehearsal;
2. Musicians practise their own parts away from the rehearsal;
3. The song is sung *to* the congregation;
4. The song is introduced to the congregation with the expectation of them joining in.

Let us look at each of these different elements in turn.

The Musicians are Introduced to the New Song in a Rehearsal

This gives the music leader the chance to acquaint the musicians with *why* the song was chosen and its relevance to the life of the church at this point. Attention should be paid to the words, and musicians should be encouraged not to be too quick to play or sing, but to read and absorb the words they will be using. This can be done by each person reading in silence, by different individuals reading several lines or a verse of the hymn, by reading together in chorus or antiphonally.

Being a keyboard player, Janet has sometimes played the song through several times, but asked the musicians simply to read the words as the song is played. Once in a workshop she encouraged us all to read through the words of *Ye Holy Angels Bright* and to identify which was the climactic line, which everything else was leading to or flowing from. We identified 'assist our song' as this centre point. It then raised the question as to why we need that help. This was considered to be a radically new approach to words, which in turn affected how they were accompanied. On another occasion one of the guitarists commented that she did not usually look at the words, but just played the notes. It is important to understand that the music is not an end in itself, but a vehicle to convey words of praise, confession, dedication, trust, faith and so on. Therefore, the music should draw our attention to the words, not to itself.

The music should draw our attention to the words, not to itself

Once musicians are familiar with the words they are using in the new song, they can begin to add their voices and instruments. It is at this point that the basic geography of the song should be taught. This means becoming familiar with the layout of the written music and/or words and the sequence in which the whole should be played or sung. For example, where are the repeats? Where does the refrain come? Is there a bridge? What does the intro look like, and what about the outro? How many verses are there? How do we get from the end of one verse or chorus to the beginning of the next (what we call the 'turnaround')? Are there any parts of the song that are too hard for this group of musicians or congregation? Are there any modifications which need to be made to make it more congregation-friendly? How would we usually expect to play this song?

Working through these different elements will eventually enable the musicians to understand the song and agree the way they would usually play it. This becomes the default mode. Having a default mode that is known and used by all the musicians means not having to reinvent how the song is done each time it is chosen. It also means that the congregation know what to expect, and they can participate with confidence. This does not preclude introducing changes to harmony or style at a later stage, as outlined in the section on 'Making it Special,' but these changes can build on the known and are then more likely to be well received by the congregation.

Here are some of the technical terms used for different parts of contemporary songs:

Intro: instrumental material used before the vocals come in to help people start at the same time. This should clearly set the key and the tempo of the song (and mood).

Outro: instrumental material which rounds off the song once the lyrics have finished. Use with caution, since long outros leave the congregation with nothing to do.

Turnarounds: instrumental material linking different sections of the song. We distinguished between...

Chorus to verse turnarounds, and
Chorus to chorus turnarounds, which in some songs are different.

Bridge: a section usually in the middle of the song which may bring in a different tune or feel and lyrics.

Pre-chorus: some songs have a line or two at the end of each verse which lead into the chorus proper. An example would be the line 'All within me falls at your throne' in *King of Kings, Majesty.*

Coda: a sung portion only used once at the very end of the song, often a repeated last line or extra chorus.

These basics can be decided when the song is being learned at rehearsal, and everyone will then be clear what the introduction is like and when to start singing. They will also be able to navigate themselves around the song and know how it will finish. It is important to consider the vocal range of the song, whether it is very high or very low and whether this is within the capability of these particular musicians and this congregation. Linked with this is what is the best key for the song. For example, is it in a key which is compatible for both guitar and keyboard if used together, and what does this mean for solo instruments, especially those which transpose?

Clarity of introductions is important for the congregation, especially if there are a range of different groups of musicians involved on different Sundays. An ambiguous introduction means the congregation are hesitant to sing as they are anxious about being embarrassed if they start too soon. It is the role of the musicians to serve the congregation and facilitate their singing, including making it clear when the congregation should come in. Sometimes this will mean sacrificing personal preferences in order to provide a supportive lead. The job of the musicians is to draw the congregation's attention to God and worship of him, not themselves.

It is also worth mentioning at this point that the way an organist introduces a hymn is usually different from the way a music group will introduce a song. Often a hymn is introduced by playing the first or last line with a short space before the first verse starts. This pause occurs at the beginning of every new verse. On the other hand, songs are usually more rhythmically driven, and so any introduction and links between verses remain within the continuous beat of the song. When hymns are led by a music group, the way the hymn is played is by keeping a steady rhythm between verses. There may be an instrumental turnaround between the verses to give the congregation an opportunity to draw breath, but the music continues and leads into the next verse. This can be a particular problem for those trained as organists who now find themselves playing more contemporary keyboard music—there is often a steep unlearning curve to negotiate.

Many contemporary songs are composed in an aural tradition

At the point of introducing new material it is important to consider the style of the song. There are a number of ways in which a song can be made special and these are discussed later on, but when a new song is being introduced it is important to decide initially what style will be used. This is where it is important to understand the competence and skill of the musicians in any ensemble. Many contemporary songs are composed in an aural tradition and are not easy to convey accurately with written notation. They often have more emphasis on rhythm than melody, with vocal line and instrumental accompaniment both syncopated. The skill needed by a music leader is to match the intended feel and style of the song with the skill and competence of the members of the group, and indeed the ability and expectation of the congregation.

Musicians Practise Their Own Parts at Home

As you can see from the detail outlined in the section above, much preparatory work needs to be done in introducing new material. Making best use of rehearsal time for musicians requires direction and focus. Each music leader should know the abilities of the members of the group so as to plan for each person's contribution to complement what the musicians produce in combination. Once the basics of the song or hymn are understood by the musicians as a group, individuals need to practise their own contribution at home.

This means that for vocalists, the words can become familiar and difficult intervals or rhythms can be practised. For instrumentalists, the song becomes part of the muscle memory—fingers become familiar with specific chord progressions or note sequences so that at upcoming rehearsals the hymn or song can be easily worked on further in the group. For solo instruments, this provides an opportunity to work on a part which complements but does not duplicate the tune. In most contemporary Christian music recordings the melody is usually left to the vocalist, with solo instruments playing a complementary line or playing in the spaces between the lines of the verses. This way, when a solo instrument enters, it brings a freshness to the song, perhaps highlighting specific words. If all the instruments in a music group play all the time, and mostly duplicating the tune, this results in a muddy, indistinct sound.

Each musician needs to add something of value to the song, rather than just playing along. Personal practice time enables musicians to be confident and secure about what their contribution is in that song, and to be well prepared for the next rehearsal. It may be that there are several group rehearsals where a new song or hymn is worked on, with opportunities for individual practice in between, but eventually it will be time to begin to introduce the song to the congregation.

The Song is Sung to the Congregation

The group and individual rehearsals should have ensured that everyone knows how the piece works, who is playing what and when, what the agreed introduction is and that the vocalists are secure in knowing when to come in. A good test of whether the music group or choir is ready to introduce new material is if they can manage to sing or play it with only a glance at their music. They should be familiar enough with their part only to need it for prompts.

Once the new piece has been practised and everyone knows what they are doing, they will be ready to sing this to the congregation so that they have heard it a few times before being expected to join in. This might be before or after the service, although depending on the type of church, this might be drowned out by the congregation talking. Alternatively a new song could be sung to the congregation during communion, when they are likely to be quieter, in a more reflective mood and so ready to listen. Obviously, some songs or hymns might be too upbeat and rousing for this particular place in the service. However, the idea is that the congregation has had the opportunity to hear the new material on several occasions before being expected to join in. Therefore, when they do sing it for themselves it is not completely unknown. You may need to be creative about what this looks like within the structure of your own services.

The Song is Introduced to the Congregation with the Expectation of Them Joining In

After the musicians have worked on new material as a group, individuals know and have practised their parts and the song has been sung to the congregation several times, it is then time for the congregation to be encouraged to join in singing the song. There are a number of ways this may happen depending on the difficulty of the piece and the nature of the congregation as well as the lead given by the musicians.

If the song or hymn is relatively simple, it may be that the congregation can sing along as the musicians lead. Another approach is that the musicians sing either the first verse or the whole of the piece while the congregation listens and follows the words. They will then sing as the song is repeated. There is much to recommend this approach as it enables the congregation to engage with the words first and then the music.

A more formal approach would be for the song to be specifically taught to the congregation. This allows the music leader to pick up on a difficult rhythm or interval and help the congregation to know how to sing that phrase or line. It is common for congregations to even out syncopation, so a skilful music leader will need to decide how much this matters, and how much to accommodate this tendency. However, this 'hymn practice' approach only works well if the congregation are willing to receive this way of learning new songs. It depends on a good relationship between the music leader and the congregation and requires time to be allocated in or before the service.

In this digital age, some churches email online links for songs they are about to introduce to the congregation. People can then listen to them at any time that suits them. The danger of this approach is that the congregation will learn the song as provided on YouTube, but the musicians in church may not be able (or indeed willing) to reproduce this exactly and may therefore have made some changes or adaptations. Having provided a range of options as to how new songs can be introduced to the congregation, it is up to the skill of the music leader who knows the congregation, knows the song and how the musicians play it, to make the choice which best fits their church situation. Once a new song is introduced to the congregation it is then helpful for the song or hymn to be regularly incorporated into services for a few weeks. This enables it to become part of the bank of material regularly drawn upon for congregational use.

Maintenance—Practising for Sunday

4

This will be the shortest section of this book, since this is probably what you do already. But it is worth asking some questions, which might help you to think again about how you actually rehearse. We begin with the team, including musicians and any tech team members. You probably already open with a prayer, but to give time to praying together, for one another's needs or for the coming service, will be time well spent. Some bands also spend time looking together at a Bible passage, perhaps that which will be used on Sunday, or maybe a passage from which one of the songs you will be using is taken. These God-centred rather than music-centred activities will help to bind you together, and lift you from merely being a bunch of people to being leaders of worship.

The Role of Rehearsals

Obviously time will always be a pressure, so the question of discipline can usefully be addressed. We have worked with three rules: turn up; tune up; and shut up. A rehearsal is not to be used for setting up or tuning: that should all be done beforehand. That is tough on drummers and easier for flautists, but out of love for one another you will not want to waste people's precious time because of your own unpreparedness. Neither are rehearsals for learning your own parts. In one of John's churches people were given permission to challenge other band members with the command 'Stop twiddling!' if they were playing to themselves while someone was speaking or trying to work on something which did not involve them. This was done in a light-hearted way, but was highly effective in saving time and focusing attention. Singers particularly need to keep quiet while instrumental parts are being developed.

The mechanics of how you know what hymns and songs are to be used in any service will vary from church to church, but it is obviously a good idea if you do know before you turn up to the service. The maintenance time during your rehearsal is then about how you will use the song in that particular service. Will you stick to the song's default mode, which you established when you first learnt it? Or are there circumstances which mean you might want to do something different? It is worth asking when exactly the song will come in the service and how it is expected to function. A breezy opening to gather people and focus on God will probably feel different from a meditative song during communion, but some songs might function differently depending on how you treat them. So how are you going to handle each song or hymn?

If it has been a while since you used a song, you will need to make sure that everyone remembers the default mode, understands the geography of the song, knows how you will use repeats, first and second time bars, DSs and DCs and so on (ask a trained musician if you are unfamiliar with these terms). But then look for the important, and therefore dangerous parts. For many bands, practising a song is merely about bashing through all five verses from start to finish, but this might not be the best way. Once a song is underway there is little which can go wrong, but misplay the intro or the turnaround and the congregation can be left uncertain and the entries messy. This will simply distract people and break the flow of worship. So make sure you are as tight as can be about how you will bring people in, both at the start and for each section.

How Congregations Learn

Remember too that congregations usually feel their way into songs in four-beat and two-bar sections. They might not be able to explain that this is what they do, or know the correct musical terminology, but that is just what feels right for them. So beware of the idiosyncratic arrangements you find in some hymn or song books where extra bars are either inserted or omitted. Just because a printed music book says something, that does not mean that you have to play it that way. Your job is to make worship as easy as possible for the people, not to confuse them. So you need to put much more work into what you do *between* the verses, so that the verses will take care of themselves.

Your job is to make worship as easy as possible for the people, not to confuse them

You also need to practise sets, rather than songs. If you use a series of songs together, rather than a 'hymn sandwich' approach where songs stand alone, you will need to think about how you maintain the flow of worship, and how you transition smoothly from one song to the next. Our approach was to make sure that someone was always playing during a set, maybe a synth or string pad, or some gentle piano arpeggios. If your model involves the worship leader speaking out or praying between songs, this can be done as a voice-over, rather than merely announcing the next song during a silence marred only by the frantic rustling of pages. Of course there will be times when you deliberately want to use a period of silence, but this should be done deliberately, and not merely because no-one can think of anything to play. So your songs need to be seen and rehearsed in context.

You will also pay attention to any difficult bits. Rather than simply playing through a song, listen for parts where people constantly get it wrong, and go back over and over it until you have ironed out the problem. Expunge the term 'That will do!' from your vocabulary, and make sure there are no issues left which, again, might distract the congregation from their worship. And remember that the maintenance time is not for individual practice, or for learning new songs. It is simply to polish up the music so that your use of it in the service is appropriately perfect, or as John Piper advocates, strive for 'undistracting excellence.'[4]

5 Development Part 2: Making it Special

So you have thoroughly learned your material, and you all know its default mode—how you will play it in the absence of any further directions to the contrary. Now begins the really exciting part of any rehearsal time: raising the level of what you do from competent to brilliant! This material is based on some work that John did on music and emotion. Why is it that for some people certain musical events can trigger emotional reactions, such as tears, or even physical ones, such as tingles down the spine? Is there anything we might do to heighten the possibilities of such experiences among the worshippers?

Before we go any further, though, we need to stop and ask whether or not that is a good thing to do. In John's book on Vineyard worship he noted that because of the Vineyard churches' theology of intimacy with God, anything musically interesting is deliberately edited out, lest the gaze of worshippers is diverted from the face of Jesus onto those of the musicians.[5] And if musicians know (as we do) how to help people towards emotional reactions, is that not manipulation, and therefore inappropriate in worship settings? Let us hold those two questions, simply noting them for now, as we consider what exactly it is which can trigger emotion.

What emerged clearly from John's research is that emotion is most commonly triggered by the unpredictable. We have all heard enough Western tonal music that even if we would not describe ourselves as musicians we still know subconsciously how music works. Any song which does exactly what we would expect it to do is unlikely to trigger much reaction. Even if the words touch us, the music will not. But if the music does something unexpected, it will wake us up and grab our attention. To illustrate this, let us look again at a song we quoted from earlier. The normal harmonization of verse 3 goes like this:

But it is possible to reharmonize those dramatic words in different ways, for example:

This immediately adds drama and interest to the words. Music works by using these kinds of surprises judiciously, giving a much greater impact. If every verse were harmonized in the same way, there would be no sense of surprise, and nor would those new chords necessarily enhance the words.

It follows, therefore, that in terms of music being interesting, the worst possible adjective you could use to describe it would be 'predictable.' So what might we do with our songs and hymns to give them that extra interest, and possibly to touch the worshippers more deeply? And, again, should we?

Let us return to that word 'manipulation.' We hear it as a negative thing, subtly making people do what we want them to, against their wills. But actually the root meaning is 'to handle skilfully.' Only secondarily does it have any negative connotations. The fact is that skilfully or not, musicians do 'handle' people, and they also handle the musical content. We have all been to church services which we would describe as boring. We did not go wanting to be bored, but the way that the music, in this case, was handled, left us feeling bored. Leaders do not have a choice whether we affect people or not, but we do have in our leading the possibility of helping people into boredom or into excitement. Another factor is that as leaders of worship we do respond to what the congregation is doing, so this is not a one-way street: it is much more of a reciprocal relationship.

Secondly, it has to be said that an emotional experience is not the same as an encounter with God, but it can be a gateway for such encounters, as the creativity of God is celebrated in the creativity of the music and the musicians. The deliberate playing down of musical creativity in Vineyard worship sounds very spiritual, but is ultimately world-denying. So we would argue that for the music to be led creatively is a positive thing which can enhance the experience of worship for the congregation. It is also worth noting that it is good for the musicians too to be stretched. Nobody wants to be led in worship by musicians who are already bored.

Three Approaches to Musical Creativity

In our work together we developed three different approaches to this creative time in our rehearsals, *song-based, skills-based* and *team-based*. In a song-based workshop we would take a song we knew well, and ask the question 'How might we do this differently?' What might we add to the song to make it more interesting, or what musical surprises might we add? Take as an example a carols by candlelight service in one of John's churches. We used the well-known carol *Hark! The Herald Angels Sing*, but played the three verses differently: one straight, one reggae and one with a kind of Status Quo shuffle. This worked because in each case what the congregation were singing did not vary at all. It was only accompaniment which changed underneath the tune. So might we give a song an appropriate but different feel from the ubiquitous soft rock of the worship-song culture, but do so in a way which would not confuse the congregation?

A good first step is to spend time learning to listen deeply to a recording of a song in order to understand what is going on. One great track to analyze like this is *The Lord is gracious and compassionate*, which you can find on YouTube here: https://www.youtube.com/watch?v=7Xzk9qtlvuo. Listen carefully to see which instruments are doing what, and when. In particular, listen to when they are *not* playing. The universal tendency in worship bands is for everyone to play all the time (and usually all to play the same thing), but this track demonstrates how the principle 'less is more' really is a helpful one. This is vital, since it is easy for us to feel that unless we are playing constantly it is not worth us bothering to get out of bed. This kind of deep listening shifts our focus from 'me' to 'us,' and helps us realize that the overall band sound is more important than our own performance, and that we need a highly developed servant heart.

The universal tendency in worship bands is for everyone to play all the time

Then we can listen to learn about new styles. Let us use reggae as an example. There is at least one reggae-style worship song, dating from the mid-1980s, so why not more? You could begin by simply listening together to some classic reggae songs, and asking what is going on. You will soon notice that the guitarist is not strumming all the way through: he is playing stabs on beats 2 and 4 of each bar, as is the organist. Then you will hear that the bass is not playing at all on beat 1, as is usual, but coming in on beat 2, and then spending most of the bar on the dominant, note 5 of the scale, rather than the tonic or root note. The bass tends to play in patterns of two bars rather than one. The drums are different too: the main kick-drum beat in each bar comes on beat 3, not 1 and 3 as is usual. The snare drum is probably played with the snares switched off, giving a kind of tambour sound. If there are other instruments, listen and try to identify what they are doing. It is this mixture of different instrumentation which gives reggae its distinctive sound, and once you understand that, you can begin to experiment with songs you know well to see what might work with this new feel, and with the resources you have available. It can be very difficult for guitarists used to constant strumming to learn to play just two stabs per bar, so you can move on to the individual practice at home until you have all mastered the style. Then you can add it to your possible repertoire.

You may not feel that your congregation is quite ready for Bob Marley, of course, but the principle underneath this is that to learn to play in different styles you can listen closely to recordings in order to understand their distinctives, and then practise until you can begin to play them. This is of course more difficult than simply turning up on a Sunday knowing that nothing out of the ordinary will be demanded of you, but it is also much more rewarding, will help individuals to grow in skill, and can be great fun in the early stages where you hilariously mess it all up!

Another way to approach a song is by the route of reharmonization. Most worship songs use simple major and minor chords (and precious few of them), but a session listening to some jazz recordings will demonstrate that there are more than four chords in the universe, and that some of them sound quite nice in the right contexts. Some knowledge of music harmony will come in helpful here, but again it can be great fun experimenting. In an earlier book John made some suggestions about what you might do with *In Christ Alone* and *Be still for the presence.*[6] As a very simple start, you might try replacing dominant 7th chords with dominant 11^{ths}. Instead of a D7 chord in the key of G, use what jazz musicians would call C over D (written C/D), in other words a C major triad over a D bass note. For a bit of added tension you could even try moving to a C diminished over D (C°/D) before resolving back to the G major. Again, individual instrumentalists can practise in their own time to build up a much greater repertoire of chords, along with the knowledge of when it might be good to use them, so that when you meet as a band different members will have something new to contribute to the whole. This kind of reharmonization of some of the verses of hymns is *de rigeur* in the cathedral choral tradition, when the final verse is given a whole new treatment in order to bring the hymn to an exciting climax. We have not heard many people complaining about manipulation in that context!

Modulation is another well-tried technique, when the last verse is transposed up, usually by one tone, to add to the sense of excitement. A song such as *Great is the Darkness* works well, as the modulation reinforces the building sense of triumph in the words. You will then need to rethink the turnaround: as a general rule the dominant, or 5th, chord of the key *you are going to* will help people to make the leap:

```
G              C           D   G   (D/E, E7)  A          D
Pour out your Spirit on us today              Great celebrations...
```

Obviously all this can be overdone. That is why cathedral organists usually only fiddle around with the final verse, maybe one in four or five. The principle of 'expectancy violation' means that you have to build up expectancy and then violate it in order to add interest for the congregation. Most of the time we operate with no violation, so that songs are predictable, but it can be equally bad practice never to build up any expectancy by making things different every time.

As you might imagine it can be great fun and tremendously rewarding to give yourselves permission to experiment and try to do things differently. Evolutionary scientists tell us that only around 1.3% of mutations are beneficial, so that most of them simply die out, and if that is true of your musical experimentation, at least you will have had fun trying. But when you hit that wonderful 1% it can really bring your worship to life.

All this may sound quite technical and instrument-based, so remember the simple beauty of occasional *a capella* singing, or of deliberately using harmony if that is not your normal tradition.

A skills-based approach will focus not on making a particular song better, but rather on making the musicians better. It might be a masterclass on helping solo instruments to play better by not playing the tune, but playing *between* lines of/phrases of the tune, or between verse and refrain. So the old song *Great is the Lord,* can be enhanced if, say, a flute does not play the line everyone is singing, but simply adds the little fills between the lines:

It can be the case that weaning instrumentalists off the tune is the hardest part, but once you have grasped the idea that the congregation are providing the melody, you can be set free to play something different.

In one of John's churches we used two keyboards, and at first the temptation was for them both to try to play everything together. So we held a workshop on second keyboards. They were not there simply to replicate the main piano part, but could add other ingredients into the mix. They could replace solo instruments, for example by playing the flute part above if there was no actual flute. They could add the bass line in the absence of a bassist, or thicken the sound out with a string or synth pad, simply holding sustained chords. They could add horn stabs, or they could add a Hammond organ sound around the piano part to replicate Black Gospel music. Many keyboards can even be used in place of a drum kit. We spent time as a team experimenting with different sounds and helping our keyboard players to learn new ways of playing. We found that achievement of a good second keyboard style helped the principal keyboard to be less busy.

Vocals could be used differently too. Giving people space to try working out their own harmonies can be very effective, but you could also experiment further, for example by learning to sing Black Gospel, where, due to lack of hymn books, the leaders would sing out the next line just before the congregation needed it, or provide a kind of foundation of the tune so that soloists could improvise around it. We dare to suggest that many church choirs would find this a far more exciting way of singing!

Of course there are many many different musical genres, so if none of those we have mentioned seem to resonate with your church's style, maybe you could use the principles behind this section and make them more your own. A church with a wide mix of people and ages demands a much richer musical diet than is usually evident.

A church with a wide mix of people demands a richer musical diet

And finally, development can happen simply by *team-building*. A fascinating study analyzes one church's musical life and identifies the huge gap between the sort of music band members chose to listen to in their own time and the music which the church allowed them to use on Sundays.[7] In one of John's churches time was given over during rehearsals not just for praying and worshipping together, but also for individual members to bring along a favourite track and to talk about why this music meant so much to them. Not only did this generate some transferable ideas for their worship music, but it also helped people to get to know others and what was important to them musically.

Postscript: 'You Must be Kidding!'

John's son and his wife are young, busy rising executives in the Netherlands, with a young daughter. They play in the worship band at their local church. When John told Paul about this book, his immediate reaction was as above. How can you expect busy people to give this much time to practice in a twenty-first-century yuppie world? Like so many musicians, they would simply turn up maybe an hour before a service and bash through the material they would soon be playing. His comment is understandable, but our response was that in our experience the band practice was the highlight of the week, an exciting chance to be together, to hone our musical skills and to play more effectively and creatively. We really looked forward to those evenings. Our hunch is that to shift our mindset from 'How little can we get away with to make a joyful noise on Sunday?' to 'How much can we possibly invest to make the worship of our brothers and sisters as wonderful as possible?' will not only take our church worship to a new level, but will also be fulfilling for us. Change begins with that shift of attitude, and we hope that we have not trodden on too many toes, but that the toes we have encouraged you to dip into the water in this booklet will encourage you to take the plunge.

Notes

1 There is material around which can help with this process. See chapters by J Witvliet and F Burch Brown in C Kroeker (ed), *Music in Christian Worship* (Collegeville, MN: Liturgical Press, 2005). See also C Patterson, *How to Learn Through Conflict* (Grove Pastoral booklet P 96) and E Jordan, *Honest Conversations in Churches* (Grove Pastoral booklet P152).

2 M Earey, *How to Choose Hymns and Songs for Worship* (Grove Worship booklet W 201)

3 J Leach, *Hymns and Spiritual Songs* (Grove Worship booklet W 132).

4 J Piper, 'What Unites us in Worship,' https://www.desiringgod.org/articles/what-unites-us-in-worship, 2003 (accessed 13 June 2023).

5 J Leach, *Encountering Vineyard Worship* (Grove Worship booklet W 228).

6 J Leach, *Wisdom for Worship Bands* (Grove Worship booklet W 239).

7 M Porter, 'Marginal Musical Spaces at St Aldates, Oxford,' *Journal of Contemporary Religion*, 31:2, 239-53. Available online: https://doi.org/10.1080/13537903.2016.1152680 (2016).